Circumstantial Voice

By

Ginger Meeder

This book is a work of fiction. Places, events, and situations in this story are purely fictional. Any resemblance to actual persons, living or dead, is coincidental.

ISBN: 1-4107-2752-1 (e-book)
ISBN: 1-4107-2753-X (Paperback)

Library of Congress Control Number: 2003091385

This book is printed on acid free paper.

Printed in the United States of America
Bloomington, IN

1stBooks - rev. 06/19/03

Acknowledgements

I believe in gratitude to which I have been graced and blessed with oceans of. Sometimes it is difficult thanking those that are closest to us and my husband is no exception. You my dear, have given me more than words can convey, so I thank you for being the person you are. My cousin-sister, Sue, you have been a true spirited friend and constant support for my writing and I cannot thank you enough. I would like to be stuck on a desert island with you so we could write one hell of a comedy script. You rock! A special thank you to Jon, who helped me write the French subtitle to my poem, "A Lover's Musings of Pleasures Lost." Especially, since I do not speak a word of French. Thank you, Kimmy, who had the courage to breathe the muse into me for, "Battered Blessed." Humorists such as Sammy Levenson, Erma Bombeck, for the entertaining writing wit they composed.

My appreciation to you the reader, for reading and buying my poetry book, you are owed gratitude for your loyalty and support. And that means you rock!

Circumstantial Voice

Vignette of a Poetic Spirit

When power leads man towards arrogance, poetry reminds him of his limitations. When power narrows the areas of man's concern, poetry reminds him of the richness and diversity of his existence. When power corrupts, poetry cleanses. For art establishes the basic human truth which must serve as the touchstone of our judgment.

—-John F. Kennedy

CONTENTS

Chapter 1
Earthly Savorings (light & airy slices of poetry pie)

Porch Settin.. 4
Poetic Eyes 6
Chloe`...7
Shall We?.. 10
Corn Dance..13
Edge of Winter 15
Seasonal Sonata 16
Wintry Scheme...17
Blessings of A Tree 20
Dreamer's Petition 22
Seashore Reflections 24
The Laundromat 27

Chapter 2
Soul Swimming(the deep thinking stuff, WARNING, you can either sink or swim)

Battered Blessed (Supplication) 31
A Childless Woman's Cries Unto Heaven.................... 33
Employment Blues.. 36
Cruelty Of Age 38
Wallflower 41
The Family Farm Eulogy.. 44
The White Granite Cross.. 47
Without a Trace.. 49
Black Hearse 50
Lamentations 52
Absence Of Innocence... 53
Venomous Tongues.. 55
Highway Prophecy 57

Chapter 3
We interrupt Circumstantial Voice for a Haiku/Senryu Moment...
(Please stay tuned, your Haiku/Senryu selection as follows

Summer Finale` 60
Melancholy... 61
Torments of a Homeless Man 61
Put Down Artist 61
Ocean's Kiss 62
Liar, Liar 62
Supernatural Prayer 62
Fireworks 63
Sheer Lunacy 63
When Enemies Meet.. 63
Mea culpa... 64
Heaven On Earth 64
The Lonely Blessed 64
Beyond Vengeance... 65
Disturbing Contemplation.. 65
Rustic Ritual 66
End of the Line 66
Walk in My Shoes 66

Chapter 4
Not for the Faint of Heart
This is the chapter that your mother warned you about

Small Talk 68
Interlude 69
Transgressions... 70
Lover's Storm 71
A Lover's Musings Of Pleasures Lost 73
Confessions.. 75
Regrettably... 76
A Moment of Passion... 78
Whisper Your Secrets 80

For Rachel Beth

October 2, 1986-February 12, 2003

Chapter 1

Earthly Savorings (light & airy slices of poetry pie) This chapter is exactly what the descriptive sentence states. You aren't going to become tarnished by reading any of this stuff. You simply won't have to work too hard at it, okay? Okay. My stress-free poetry.

"If it falls your lot to be a street sweeper, sweep streets like Michelangelo painted pictures, like Shakespeare wrote poetry, like Beethoven composed music; sweep streets so well that all the host of Heaven and Earth will have to pause and say, Here lived a great sweeper, who swept his job well."

Martin Luther King, Jr.

Porch Settin

Lets set for a spell on the front porch you and I

So we can count all the cars, people and animals that pass us by

Allow the sun's golden rays to melt into our eyes

Listen to the air whisper through the North Carolina Pines

Behold the trees as they sway from side to side

With new leaves of spring green to enchant our eyes

Sit yourself down we've no secrets to hide

There is nowhere else I'd rather be than by your side

I'll sit on the top step with you nestled in rocking chair fold

As we await the spring spectacular to explicate & grow

What lies before us is what GOD started from seed

A magnificent natural heavenly mystery

This season of year is consequently compelling

What awakens next is so mystically storytelling

I look to the sky as clouds roll before me

Billowy white clouds with splatters of blue that enrapture lyrically

Birds stream by with secrets their not telling

Insects creak & croak with melodies all knowing

No wonder this place holds one captive and spellbound

It seduces you to be held prisoner from its unaffected whimsy's &

charms

Silence of wonderment & pitch black star laden night skies

Bestow rhapsodic awe in one's soul of eyes

Such beauty exists under North Carolina skies

Consider, as true twill be difficult to utter goodbye

"This Side of Heaven" is extraordinarily no lie.

Poetic Eyes

Wrinkle blessed niche of eyes

Gently speak of wisdom beyond

Your well seasoned soul

Relevantly positioned,

In its proper centered place

Weather beaten creases line

A life stained skin and face

Abiding innocence strongly evident

Running its course

Within the lines

Time painting artistry of age

Crinkled nose would suggest

You know some secrets

While many ignorantly

Re-read over the same life pages

Time and time again

Chloe`

I dreamt that I misplaced my Chloe` today.

My sister's child who boldly stakes a claim on my heart

There was a sense of sorrow paired with fear.

How could I have lost her?

Chloe`! Chloe`!

I call her name sharply into the air of apprehension.

I step up to the counter and say, "Where is that child?"

This is so irresponsible of me and at this age?

And than it occurs to me,

What this dream has really said

My inner child is now dead.

My soul cries out through the pores of my head

I rapidly approach my coming of age

My mind, heart and soul fight to the end

I resolutely choose to not walk that path.

The telephone rings.

I awake with a start

And a smile of affirmation,

Chloe` is here safe within my heart

As is the re-awakening of my inner child again

This revelation brings a smile to my heart and soul.

I wipe the sleep from my eyes

And all of me concludes,

To ride my bike,

Blow bubbles to the wind,

Pitch a giggle fit or two.

Never you mind that silly dream again, you fool.

The author with her pride and joy, her awesome bike, back in the

70's.

Shall We?

Shall we dance among the brilliant stars tonight?

Let us capture the love we know under the moon's light

As we discover the essence of love

that grows with each passing of night

We are bound together as one with no thought to take flight

Our love has known strong and weak

Words fall from my lips to caress yours as you speak

I cannot imagine my life with or without you as we laugh

Memories flash before us in black & white

of times we thought our vows would not last

But our strength to hold on has remained steadfast

We balance one another more now than in our past

I am amazed by this quiet love that we have that has grown

The paths we took misguided,

our arms entwined into the unknown

Wisdom gained, lovers quarrels, misjudgments

angry words spun across the rooms carelessly

Allowing ourselves to be who we are as purely the facts

Love is not shallow, unfriendly nor unkind,

but quiet, always in time

With the stars, the moon,

black painted evening sky

So again I say,

Shall we dance amongst the brilliant stars tonight?

Of course we shall,

until the sun's full rise into daylight.

g. meeder

Corn Dance

The season's corn has again grown taller than I

Leafy and green,

Tasseled out stalks

Pointed vein centered leaves

Bend for miles in a sea of maize

Indian myths soliloquize in nature's song

Through the curvature of the leaves

Corn's resilient presence

Ancient symbolic bounty

Harvest season's inescapable advance

Subtle suggestions hint

In the sunrises, sunsets

Night skies, summer's breeze

Fragrance of air mentions

Corn's mystical incidence

Present in every wave

Of the corn sashay

I walk throughout its esoteric sanctum

Golden hair predicts ears readiness

Leaves mingle amongst the sisterhood

Mischievously teasing one another sing-song

Who will produce the most tender of ears?

So amidst the corn echelon of harmony I dance

Vigilantly awaiting their response per chance

Edge of Winter

Prismatic waiting eyes glow impatient

Inside crystal frosted windowpanes

Children huddle together waiting

Ominous clouds lurk overhead

While winter skies laugh

Releasing wet sloppy gigantic snowflakes

That lay crumpled on early spring green grass

Creaking door bursts forth

Children tumble onto the front yard

Effervescent breath circles dance about their heads

Boundless energy explodes into a snowball,

Fight of fights

The edge of winter,

Earthly reprieve delight

Seasonal Sonata

Natural Jewel

Autumn leaves falling

Seasons change calling

Air is breezy

Sky a cloud studded blue

For artistry of color

Explodes before you

This time of year,

A natural jewel...

Wintry Scheme

Land & Sea Stormy

Winter's spirit angered fury

Unleashed in blizzard hiss

Serene sunlit morning diamonds glisten

Delicately frosted snowfall blankets ground

Intimate kitchen window viewing

Winter sighs a bittersweet kiss

Earth's soul has spoken,

Mother Nature squalls and murmurs

Spring's ardent arrival is next

Spring Dance

Lime green ocean of budding trees

Color brilliance teases eyes

Spring of soul implores

Visionary splendor has fallen upon us at long last

Fuchsia purple anger painted sky

Uneasy calm silence rests

White jagged lightning bolt

Pierces blackened grumbling clouds

Disturbed wind howls and twists

Trees bow and sway in trembling fear

Cease cold northern winter hiss

Fragrance of thunderous rain reveals

Springs explosive moody ritual

Will merge into summer's glare

Steam heated sunray dance

Summer Blaze

Hazy white misted morning hush

Fully blossomed fragrances entice

Rose & honeysuckle flourish

Longer days of sunlight

Merge into evening's sunset

Radiant clouds silhouette

The sun's iridescent orb

Whimpers a perpetual retreat

Sun, Moon and Stars whisper

Leaves will turn from summer's heat

Earth's change of seasons, now complete.

Blessings of A Tree

I am a tree

Look at me

What do you see?

I have leaves of many colors

So many are the envy of me

My leaves turn colors

Maroon, coppers and golds

They will fall to the ground

As the seasons change and unfold

Than winter's wrath shall turn on me

Barren and bitter cold

Uniquely patterned snowflakes of white

Accumulate upon my forsaken branches delight

Soon spring shall blossom me out

Twigs bud, spurt and sprout

into shimmering leaves of emerald,

when spring ultimately arrives

Summer approaches with warmth and steam

My olive leaves will gleam

Glistening from the rising sun

Raindrops will sparkle after a shower has come

Earthly diamonds brilliantly reflected from the sun

All these truly are blessings you see

For a very contented tree.

(This poem is dedicated to the memory of author, Joyce Kilmer

For as you can see, I am very fond of trees)

Dreamer's Petition

Dreams weaving mists of delusions

Merging decisions among nightfall rhythms

Wispy paths toward oblivion

Drifting beliefs anchor fragments

Freely images blend emotions

Dancing in a envisage of exhilaration

An instant of chaotic thoughts enraptured

In a subconscious surreal world

Visionary ideas take flight

Unspoken into the abysmal obscure night

Sentiments within provoke

Expressions that pave the way to dreamer's message

Inexplicably distressed

Explanations non-existent

Mind, body and soul dance fickle

Amid morality of twilight

Sensual trysts intercept

Rational thought processes

Drift in and out morally

Tumultuously suppressing

Politically correct choices

Sleep induced trance is diminished

Eyelids rustle to reality

Awakening anatomical limbs stretch

Sheets extricated from slumber position

Stormy mind tenaciously petitions

What would have resulted had I slept in?

g. meeder

Seashore Reflections

The lady by the sea observed the waves splashing

Brown eyes followed seagulls dancing in the jeweled dawning

night sky

She listened as their shrill voices cried

Waves of ocean froth crashing the sand

Stood there in silence

Entranced as the day turned to evening

In front of her wisdom blessed eyes

The sand gritted air whips at her dress

The ocean represents her life no less

Problems beating down on the sandy shores

Ocean waves rushing to distance them from her

The lady sits down yielding knees to her chest

Sighs with the panoramic view that before her besets

The ocean is an infinite beast with no rest

Echoes of spirits sing from the ocean depths

The sand is cool to her senses as it surrounds her toes

The fragrance of the ocean breeze pervades her nose

The sun, a deep purplish red as it settles down with a

final glow

This is the finest splendor of God's creative artistry one

shall ever know

An unaffected seascape of magnificence

Surround the lady sitting on the seashore

The sun goes down without musical notes

The sea, tranquil,

Moonshine glistens on supple waves

Like diamonds that have set sail to sea

Unequivocally no desires to ever come back

The glimmer of the moon silhouettes the realm

Surrounding the lady who sits by the seashore

Surrealness fills her with unspeakable bliss

No other place on earth could possibly transform her more

than this

The ocean itself, she ponders there is no other remarkable

natural gift

Secrets unknown to us buried deep within its abyss

Creatures soar to it with neediness

While others retreat from it in fearfulness

It has seized all their trust in the blink of an eye

A loved one was snared into its murky eternal core

Blessing them with hate for the ocean's seduction

While the sea endures intact with few interruptions

Broken-hearted lovers proclaim the sea a place to drown

your sorrows in

Some believe that this is where life begins

Rising, hits her sandals together to separate the

sand from their soles

Hair fluttering about her face from the gentle sea breeze

that flows

She runs a mad dash and dives on in.

This is the ocean of life she gulps

As her head resurfaces on the water's top

Droplets of sea bead on her skin

Dragging her dead weighted body out from the ocean's

awakening

The woman and the sea are kindred souls that beat as one

The lady walks away from the seashore feeling better now

that she is done

Oceanic sermon has redeemed her from coming undone.

The Laundromat

I love to people watch at the Laundromat

Is there any harm to that?

Children scatter as their guardians stumble in

Baskets filled with colorful, soiled and well-worn clothes

Giggling secrets the children chase one another with

abandoned care

Until the weathered woman who stands folding her polyester

knit slacks

Crinkles her nose in disgust, with a face that might crack

Into a thousand tiny pieces as if it were glass

This woman chose to forget about life and where it begins

She disturbs the children's rambunctious energy

To bark into the humid, dryer perfumed air

"You certainly should control your children in here!"

The children's mother blows smoke into the air from a

dangling Marlboro and states,

"Who cares?!"

The glass door squeaks as a shirtless, bearded man with

kerchief saunters in

Opens a washer lid to toss all his clothes, darks & whites

together in

Digs into his butt hugging blue jeans to find no quarters to

make the washer, bump & grind

Cockily strides to the change machine

Places a crisp new five dollar bill in

The "Who Cares?" lady's children fly around the large

capacity washers bumping into him

They stand in wonder as the silver quarters fill the cup to

the rim

He smiles at their interest and hands each one a quarter to

get rid of them

"Now go on and get you little rugrats"

The Marlboro lady gruffly retorts, "You didn't say thanks to

that guy who I wish would pull up his damn shorts."

A snicker escapes from the old woman now folding her seventh

pair of polyester knit slacks

"I wish I'd the nerve to say that."

The beat up pay phone on the wall rings to shatter the

display of humor in there

A custodian strolls in with mop & bucket to a room full of

stares

"Hey lady no smokin in here!"

He proceeds to answer the ringing phone on the wall

with his distinctive southern drawl

"Who you callin? This is a laundromat you all."

I giggle to myself and inwardly announce

Now where is that last strip of bounce?

I fold my last towel into threes placing it atop of my

clothes gingerly

Snatch up my last pair of mismatched socks

Tuck my overflowing laundry basket under my arm

Mumble out loudly, "Not too many places fascinate with

such charms."

As I walk away with excitement of my return

To this continuing lifetime soap opera,

"Soap Suds with Dryer Turns..."

Chapter 2

Soul Swimming- This is the chapter where my poetry penetrates the deep thinking muse or the stuff that you can either sink or swim at reading. Not that it is too deep or over your head, (whispers this part to your soul) but it might make you think and question life, as I do too.

"Write down everything that happened, everything that is happening to you. Write down everything you think of. There is nothing else to do." —-Carol Maso

Battered Blessed (Supplication)

She'd hoped that solitude would cure her boredom

But instead it riled up her need for normalcy

Which would elude her most of her entire adult life

As it had during her dysfunctional childhood

Life never did seem nor appear quite right

Even when he began to raise his hands to her face

He stole her soul for his God blessed marital rights

In the eventuality of normalcy is when he would lash out

No warnings,

No subtle suggestions

Not even the slightest hint

Could explain his behavior

Her only response was to cry out

Through a religion that failed her

All those wasted moments on bended knee,

Praying,

And praying for what?

Just more of the same

Words of spiritual significance only reinforced

His primal release on her

The only thing now she was grateful for

Admittedly, on reverential knee

Was Thank God!

No children as the end result

For him through me.

A Childless Woman's Cries Unto Heaven

She feels cursed and so do they,

While others whisper amongst themselves,

They are Blessed,

Unlike us they said.

Their children have given them a rough time on hearts and heads.

She inhales the smell of a baby's wonderfully formed head

Her heart is remiss at what could have been shared

Gifts of laughter

Joy of a good book read,

A silly story,

Or joke, just off the top of her head.

She sits alone here instead.

Thought it was all under control in her head.

Instinct calls to her soul again,

Haunting her with the desire ever stronger now with pressing age

Heart and soul refuse to accept this childless state

Childishly ponders the thought,

"Perhaps in Heaven I will."

The naivete of a woman who is childless

Who tries to remain hopeful in a world

Built around children, couples and families

She recalls words the doctor splattered them with

"A very slim chance, if ever at all."

Walks away neither stunned nor shocked,

Readily accepts, this is life

We must somehow go on.

Friends share their children with her through chitchat

sporadically

She greedily soaks up every word they utter her way

Giggles politely at every new silly their child has learned this

day

Returns the phone to receiver with oceans filling up her eyes.

Tries vainly to blink them away with a regretful sigh

They overflow into a steady stream down her cheeks.

I am this woman who will never have these treasures in her soul

It is still not the same as having your own,

She retorts to those who say there are other options you know

A deep breath releases itself from her healthy lungs.

Oh to have child who can taste the salted ocean surf,

Feel the surge of a stormy breeze through their hair

Sand between their toes and experience life as she had.

But every day I awaken with the same dread.

When I am dead, all of me will be dead.

A silent tear escapes rolling down my virgin cheek

Where no child has blessed.

Employment Blues

Slammin those bottles into plastic or wooden wire crates

Trying so hard to keep the pace

Man this job truly frustrates!

My mind, body & soul aches

Stand on my feet for hours on end

I have to make this work, there are bills to pay my friend

I plead with myself this shall humble thee

But thoughts tumble in all over me

I think of several other places I would much rather be

Down the steel-sectioned assembly line the bottles head

towards me

The half-gallons, quarts and pints are filled with milk

individually

Color corresponding caps are placed to seal them

mechanically

Than on down the line to be dated by sensor automatically

I inspect the dates to make double damn sure they are

stamped correctly

This job is so mindless I could scream!

But I roll my eyes, we are now bottling cream

My job is no doubt any less glamorous than the ladies before

me

One loads the bottles into a funky yellow steam cleaning

machine

While the other one inspects them as they leave the machine

For cracks, fractures in the bottle necks or the few that

didn't quite come clean

My mind wanders through the entire process

A bottle falls from the line and shatters right beside me

Splatters my legs with minute flakes of glass

I am grateful the glass didn't reach my gluteus max

I pluck the tiny slivers of glass from my leg

Hose off the trickle of blood streaming down my calf

And wonder what the heck happened to me?

A high school diploma with two and half years of college

behind me

This is where I would end up at the age of forty

I return to the line and continue my plight

Of slammin those bottles into plastic or wooden wired crates

Cruelty Of Age

I went to the local Wal-Mart today

To pick up a few things for my husband to shave

There in the line in back of me

Stood an old man quite elderly

The cashier, a young black man said, "that will be 393

dollars please."

I laughed, " I know that can't be true, must be your a

tease."

He smiled broadly back at me with a wink of his eye

Here is your change ma'am,

Delivered to me with no more lies

A quarter, a dime and a penny too

He rang out the old man's laxatives,

Two boxes of ex-lax for the wifey-poo

He wore thick glasses, could barely see.

This armless man behind me

Dug into his pocket to drag his wallet out

To pay the man what he was owed for merchandise no doubt.

As I stood & watched him balance his arm

He paid the money with simple charm

I walked out the door thinking out loud

How did it happen?

What could possibly have dealt him such harm?

Not sure if I could handle life with only one arm

In the parking lot an old man passes me by

He has a sad vacant look in his black eyes

Another seasoned man that life has drained of any sparks

Oh My God, will this be me in twenty some years at the local

Wal-Mart?

What frightens me more is the sorrow of it all

These people at one time or another were vibrant

They lived life's call

I inwardly wished I could see their lives play before me

To show me where they had been or lovers they called.

If they fought in a war, their fears through it all

What people had played a part in their turn at life?

Those still standing by them through the wrong & rights

In this journey we call Life...

But I stand here ashamed of myself in a way

We treat the elderly with such disparity.

When in reality this is what will happen some day to me.

I'll walk like a ghost in a small town

Into the local Wal-Mart and lay my money down

To have people stare at me, look crossways with cruelty in

their eyes

"You are so old why don't you just lay down & die"

But instead I will shake my ancient head with a laugh,

"Same to you! Your day is coming,

Your youth will not last.

You will walk through life a spirit from the past...

Wallflower

I am the one who hides behind her eyes

Smiling regretfully at every word you speak

For every word that slithers from your pretentious lips

Dishonest manipulation

Crushes any sincere admiration

My wallflower soul may have possessed

Haunted by living in the shadow of others

Regressing into the dark corners of my thoughts

Drowning out the slightest possibility

Of ever becoming the center of attention

Wouldn't want to interrupt your shining circumstance

Bright and animated star performance, no less

A smirk curling up on the edge of my lip

Standing ovation would be in order for this

While I again hide within myself

Sequestering my soul from your egotistic hunger

An eternal need for verbal aggression at another's expense

Usually mine.

Concealing,

Hiding,

Comfortably shifting gears

Deeper into the safe realm

Of my mind's eye

Mentally photographing this ill thought moment in time

So that I may never forget

g. meeder

The Family Farm Eulogy

Blank emotionless stares

Is the only thing that remains

After a difficult decision is made

To sell the cows, the farm

Lock, stock and barrel

Secrets kept amongst themselves

As if shame were their middle names

For an economy part to blame

Short time frames are given

When employees are gathered

The news is broken to them

Some hear bits and pieces

Others feel livelihoods are shattered

Clips of conversation dispense uneasiness

And the farmer cannot believe

What verbally has fallen from his lips

A speech he had rolled around and around

Inside his head that he had thought

Perhaps might lessen their impending dread

All it has done

Is make his heart heavy as lead

Whispers and rumors abound in the community

They all within live

Few understand where the demise of this farm

Began to unravel

Thread by thread

This is our second time around

To watch a family farm die

Ours went a few years before

With barely a whimper, whim or outcry

Reality will hit when a silver trailer

Bounces onto their farmyard

Loading up cattle one by one

Hauling them down the road

The driver will keep his fingers crossed

Hopefully this will not be the plight

Of my own farm someday

Machinery and land are auctioned away

For damn near mint prices

Subdivided lots

Real estate sold off

Partnerships severed

Tension is high in the air

Biting, harsh words will be said

Lives will continue on

Eventually bitterness disappears

Into memories golden

Of a once lively farm

Now, declared DEAD.

The White Granite Cross

I kneel before a soldier's white granite cross

Run my fingers on the name etched upon it to sense the loss

For a person who fought in a war that took lives easily at

any costs

Is there ever a sound acceptable justification to this

delusion we call war?

The men and women who died for it would suggest

Yes, there was for freedom and eternal happiness

In this moment all there is underneath me on this grassy

knoll

But the shell of a human who breathed in life but are no

more

Who in their last gasp gave up their soul for peace that

would not last

Offered up their lives to a cause that some refuse to

acknowledge from the past

They lived each day on the battlefield thinking is this day

the one?

The day I die for my country and the enemy will have won

My soul for causes that were tragic and love of my country

overblown?

But all I can offer to those that lay underneath me

Is but a prayer of thanks for what you did for me

A tear is shed from within the very heart of me

I call out, " How could this entity called War have seized

so much from us?"

When all that remains now,

Are men and women in their coffins who returned to dust

Pick myself up from my kneeling position

Wipe grass from my knees with a sigh about the human

condition

If only people would listen with their hearts,

Instead of willful, misguided ambitions.

Than all these men and women would have lived their lives

In place of dying on their battlefield missions...

To all the men and women and families and friends, whose

lives were forever changed by War or Conflicts.

Without a Trace

Has there ever been a moment in time that you could not

recall your name?

In that moment did you feel fair game?

As the memory monsters that roll around inside your head

Tried desperately to sort the mumble jumble in your moment

of dread

You began to wonder what no thoughts would feel like in

death

When death's lair creeps in upon you stealing your last

breath

There are no words I can comfort with in these instances of

debate

Nothing to remove one's fear of mortality our inner souls

create

That hits you square straight in your face

Nowhere to hide, nowhere to run, these are part of life's

race

To be born, live, and die someday without a trace.

BLACK HEARSE

When I die, don't want no morbid nursery rhymes

Or spiritual ringing chimes

A crowd hanging out inside a stuffy old church

Some dry read of a bible memorial verse

Or a somber ride in a sleek and shiny black hearse

A lady in black,

With phony teardrop eyes

Digging for tissue from her overstuffed purse

Why is black associated with death as if it were some

curse?

Just a sing song tale of how I flew up and went away

To be with the Lord on my judgement day

Would much prefer his wisdom to those on earth

When I am gone, as my friends and enemies gather

I choose not to be on display in a coffin but rather

Tossed to the winds that freely blow

No bag of bones will be found buried six feet below

My friends can ride in that shiny black hearse for a

supernatural joyride

Share a bottle or two of a cheap, drunk as a skunk

wine

Perchance earn a speeding ticket they will always treasure

Since in life I accumulated several with lead foot measures

No fond farewells

No lover's tales

Just the opinion that I lived my life as well as could be

Than scatter my ashes

Whispering to me,

"May Heaven be a by far better place than earth was to

thee."

"And if you went to hell please don't come looking for me."

Lamentations

Horizons of sunsets and sunrises flood my mind

Colors of the surreal

Emblazon memories once hard to find

Diamond sheared stars

Drape the dusk sky

Flashes of people

Who have come and gone

Walk softly behind my eyes

Laughing, cooing, luminous souls

Voices from the beyond

Intensify emotional encounters

Erratic soothing sounds beckon

Situations into existence

Deep-seated thoughts turning back

Impassioned memories from death's door

Light fragrant twilight air

Whispers across my face

If only I could touch the stars

Climb them as ladders into space

And once again look upon your lovely face.

For Rachel Beth

Absence Of Innocence

A boy of nine years of age

Wandered into the neighborhood shop

Silver braided hoop hung from his left ear

A little too streetwise for a boy

Of his youthfulness

At such an underdeveloped stage

Of his life

He lied to us at first

Than chose to come clean

After confronted by a young man

Who brought out his dishonesty,

Because he himself knew this boy's

Shortcomings since they were his own

His lie to himself was simple

He'd smoked no dope

Not even one toke

But the experienced one blew his cover

Wearing an expression tight to his face

Of I know all,

"You did so, and with several others."

g. meeder

Neighborhood punks,

Trying in vain attempt

To act older than their birth given ages

Crimson stained guilt ridden cheeks simmered,

Into a recognizable, "he found me out" stupor gaze.

His head hung low,

In shame of being caught in his deniable game

All the while,

Inside my heart grieved

For a nine year old boy

Whose life would never be the same.

Venomous Tongues

Prejudice sneaks in like a snake, on its belly

Silently slithering over a sanctimonious white man's words

I bite my tongue until it is bleeding

Damn near cut off

Nobody sees my bleeding tongue

Or the strong words I want to hit them with

Shut your ugly mouths

Enough of this white man's intolerance

My mind counters,

"It is their opinions not mine"

Internally I scream, "Enough is enough!"

The voice inside my head counter attacks

After all this time one would think

Grown men would have better things to do with their time

Than to harvest prejudice maliciously

Roaming sporadically from one set of bigotry fattened lips

To another's misdirected bias

Spiraling deeper and deeper into

the never-ending hatred abyss

g. meeder

Highway Prophecy

Rolling on down the road of life

In my clothes of morally wrong and right

Mistakes I've made

Undertake the soul of religious light

A shining star disappears into twilight

Leaves me breathless

In awe of the presence

Of the holy one

Crying out to me

Unto me you should come

For it is thy will be done

Rolling on down the road of life

Losing my way

Fighting strife for strife

Struggling against principalities

Pinned beneath evil's acrimonious sword

Will I win or lose the battle?

Only in death will it be known

Rolling on down the road of life

Count your many blessings

Nirvana shall not banish

Mortality's tormentuous voice

Echoing from the eternal ire

Of Heaven or hell's bidding

Heaven's theoretical pleas

Hell's brimstone and all consuming fires

Lend themselves to conspire

Life's unanswered questions

While I continue

Rolling on down the road of life...

Chapter 3

We interrupt *Circumstantial Voice* for

a Haiku/Senryu` moment. Stay Tuned...

Haiku is a poetry form that follows a syllable pattern of, five-seven-

five.

Senryu` is clever or witty haiku that stimulates your head and soul.

"Life is not a static thing. The only people who do not change their minds are incompetents in asylums, and those in cemeteries."—Everett McKinley Dirksen

Summer Finale`

sunflowers golden

flaxen petals bowed in prayer

season's final psalm

Melancholy

crisp air breathes your name

whispering truth on my face.

your eyes I miss most

Torments of a Homeless Man

pained eyes pierce through cap

piss runs down his frozen leg

warmth for a moment

Put Down Artist

who would ever think

words from your lips would sting so?

I pray for deaf ears

Ocean's Kiss

sun rests ocean's crest

waves reach for sandy shores kiss

frothy waves bless feet

Liar, Liar

man speaks lies loosely

twisted tongue, deceitful lips

flaming soul well done

Supernatural Prayer

anguished soul weep not

final breath passed through thy lips

death's spoken, soul rests

Fireworks

blinking lights hover

silent twinkling cornfield waltz

firefly dusk church

Sheer Lunacy

screams top of her lungs

I want off of this planet

pay cab fare lady

When Enemies Meet

soldier's feet running

hearts racing palms sweating

guns with souls meet

g. meeder

Mea culpa

stinging private thoughts

words lay buried unspoken

whose mind would it change?

Heaven On Earth

clouds of angel dust

sparkle upon heaven's touch

God sighs earth sings dusk

The Lonely Blessed

afternoon silence

begets subtle loneliness

sleep simply digress

Beyond Vengeance

I understand not

why they murdered innocence?

no way to avenge

Disturbing Contemplation

my sorrow is great

words cannot reveal my wish

terrorized by hate

Dedicated to the memory of all who perished or lost their innocence

on

September 11th, 2001

g. meeder

Rustic Ritual

determined sweat brow

took some elbow grease hoe down

my garden splendor

End of the Line

monster green tractors

devour corn rows endless

my heart weeps goodbye

Walk in My Shoes

picture you are me

a lost soul tucked inside of

mortal flesh with flaws

Chapter 4

Not for the Faint of Heart:

This is the chapter that your mother warned you about.

Fantasy, sensuality, heartbreak, lust and out of the ordinary.

I dedicate this to the rebel in any of us.

"Nothing great in the world has been accomplished without passion." —George Hegel

Small Talk

My heart races in anticipation

Of your arrival

When exchanged glances

Encounter harmonious sighs

Breathless touch excites

Stimulating untamed cravings

Soul's moral nature unbalanced

By your presence

Sexually disturbing undertones

Settle below urbane dialogue

Electrically charged impatience interrupts

Pressing sexual hunger into the open

Center of my thoughts

Polite conversation rendered illegal

"Who needs this small talk?"

Interlude

Afternoon sighs across crumpled, white sheets

Discreet whispers drift through soft flowing breeze

Dangling chimes swaying hum

Rocking chair desires as two lovers

Discover each other's garden of sensual ecstasy

Passions burst forth,

Full bloom to burn bright.

Sighs of lets make love until day turns to night.

Transgressions

Not for one solitary moment

As you would have me believe

That you are not weak,

But gentlemanly strong as my mind perceives

You are but a scoundrel,

a rascal tease,

trifling in effect with the very heart of me

In gentle lover's prose you have conveyed casually

That I love you in this scandalous way

While in my heart a soul whispers

You are so wrong

It is you the misdirected rogue

Who has fallen for me

So, say what you shall

Say what you will

But this lover's heart has your secrets just spilled.

Lover's Storm

Windshield wipers swishing back and forth in rhythmic motion

Raindrops splatter the windshield in a distinct emotion

My inner soul is combating deep commotions

While my head spins from all the sensual explosions

That a heart given freely in a true lover's devotions

Has created this euphoric feeling of orgasmic proportions

A smile passes over my lips in the memory of his first kiss

Our eruption of sensual emotions that created bliss

That gave birth to our love affair

A siren wails in the distance

Moisture beads on the windshield as it did on his skin

In his moment of sensual heat when as lover's we connected

Underneath the stormy night sky where he and I begin

Our steamy caressing, passionate undressing

Kissing, touching and lover's confessing

Murmurs of ecstasy into each other's ears

Trusting souls to one another without any fears

No cares if we will be there for each other through the years

I wipe the fog that covers the driver's side window glass

Observe flashing lights on a police car by me pass

g. meeder

The tires echo with rain splashing at its wheels

Roll down the window to inhale the fragrance of rain

Sigh to myself in remission that he has made me savor life again

A Lover's Musings Of Pleasures Lost

("Un Amoureux Se Souvien Des Plaisirs Perdus")

Passion is the bravura of capricious emotions

That rarely nurtures seeds of true love and honest devotion

It is an abstract desire that many contend for

Spoken eloquently about within the very heart of romantic

folklore

How does a lover keep the fervor of desire burning?

Without the eventuality of your lover's insatiable

yearnings?

Passions are a lover's dance into exquisite ecstasy

An indulgement of oneself in an unrelenting moment of

fantasy

Those lacking it mourn its absence with virgin-like

complacency

How can I crave something that has never been a fragment of

me?

While those of us who have known it

Grieve its disappearance from our lives as a true loss of

utmost proportion.

We spend the rest of our life in pursuit of a passion that

will equal, allowing no distortions

Only to discover passion is an emotion we may not ever

recover

For we lost this glow of passion when we dismissed our

lovers

As someone we slumber with who steals the covers.

Confessions

Do you think you could ever see?

What it is you have done to me?

A lover spurned hush surrounds

My broken heart

I have allowed you to get the best of me

Although I swore to myself

You would not...

Of course you have

There's been no lingering moment of doubt

Regrettably

I was born tempestuous

But you were born cruel

To remind me of this very truth

As if I had not known

Until there was you

Your desirableness

Reached inside hidden corners

That I never knew

Existed

Until I felt compelled

To fantasize about

Your strong sensuality

The quintessence of your stunning,

magnificent frail youth

This is my crutch

I deal with it every day

My unattractiveness

But how do you deal

With your lack of a heart

Or empathetic soul?

My lust for you

Was in every way normal

I smile in spite of my anguish

To admit that not only did I

Forbiddenly, lust after you

But loved you alone is

Regrettably, my foolish shame

A Moment of Passion

There was a man who whispered to me

Subtle words of sensuality

He lathered me in them almost ritually

I could not escape him

Nor could I explain what he did to me

Truthfully I wanted that man to make love to me

With a verbal ecstasy that at times infuriated me

To rebel against my marital bliss

To question the morality of mine or his

But than again if we could have kissed

Our lives would have become a pretense of something remiss

The words of passion tumbled from his lips

Sexual tensions arose in mid air

Only to quietly clash

Suspended right there.

Never to be fully explored or truly shared

There were no true intentions that this was going to be fair

Or that either one of us were going to regard

That in the end each of us would care

Contemplation's of should we stop?

This could break somebody's heart?

While in the end we resolve to part

I walk away admittedly with the remains of our broken

hearts...

Whisper Your Secrets

Whisper your secrets to me

Breathe them softly into my ear

Share your fantasies with me

Express to me your needs

Let me know if I complete you

Confess your pleasures to my soul

Trace my lips with your fingertips

Fascinate my heart with your naturalness

Seduce my eroticism with your tenderness

Erase my doubts in a moment of your sensual ecstasy

Surrender your lips

Place them upon mine

Reward me the taste of your lips so sublime

Arouse your hands to touch whatever you please

Kiss my neck with lips of desire and wanton need

Breathe in the very essence of you and me

Memorize the sweet smell of lust

My throat moans you're the reason I breathe

No other man on earth can create in me such trust

Than the one who whispers to me

His secrets of pleasure and lust

INDEX OF PHOTOGRAPHY

My comfortable rocking chair, on the front porch, in Mantua, Ohio.
Page 3

Me and my awesome bike, Erie, Pennsylvania, early 70's.
Page 9

Cornfield, on the Alger Dairy farm, in Mantua, Ohio.
Page 12

"Strength," a Holstein bull, we raised and sold to an Amish farmer.
Page 43

Mennonite Road, on a sunny day of Summer, 2002.
Page 56

Sunflower field, Deerfield, Ohio.
Page 60

Spectacular sunset, bordering one of the many fields surrounding the house we lived in.
Page 65

Personal photograph of me at my now defunct coffee shop.
Christmas, 2001.
Author's page

ABOUT THE AUTHOR

This photo was taken on one of my many life adventures(possess a gypsy soul). I ran a small coffee shop for about a year and a couple of months. I started my business a month before the tragic events of September 11th, 2001. I hope that my poetry and photography touches you in some way. As far as the validity of the poetry, if you think the poetry is about you, it is not. In the event, that you think it is not about you, it might be. I do not profess to be a literary great, but in some way, I humbly hope that my book becomes one of the coolest books you have ever read. The song that best represents me, is written by ©Alanis Morrisette, "Front Row"®. The first cut off of her

©"Supposed Infatuation Junkie"® CD.

"I write only because there is a voice within me that

will not be still."—-Sylvia Plath, 1948

www.ingramcontent.com/pod-product-compliance
Lightning Source LLC
Chambersburg PA
CBHW030411290526
45785CB00004B/1971